Keto

*This collection of recipes is a small
window into a ketogenic diet.*

*We have tried to keep the flavor and the
satisfying feel of low-carb or no-carb dishes.*

*Avocado, cheese, and nuts will
become your best friends!*

*This is a chance to use the spiralizer you were
afraid to take out of the box. Zoodles forever!*

Contents

Photos are for inspiration only.

Keto

Almond Bread

The extra egg whites help make this bread fluffy.

Serving Size

1 loaf

Ingredients

2 egg whites

2 whole eggs

2 cups almond flour

1/4 cup (1/2 stick) butter, melted

1/4 cup psyllium husk powder

1 1/2 tsp baking powder

1/2 tsp xanthan gum

1/4 cup sunflower seeds

pinch of salt

1/2 cup warm water

1/4 cup sesame seeds

Directions

1. Preheat oven to 350°F. Line a loaf pan with parchment paper and spray with non-stick cooking spray.

2. Beat the eggs and egg whites together in a large bowl.

3. Add almond flour, butter, psyllium husk powder, baking powder, xanthan gum, sunflower seeds, salt, and water to the bowl. Blend until you have a smooth dough. Don't overmix.

4. Pour the mixture into the prepared loaf pan and generously sprinkle sesame seeds on top.

5. Bake for 45 minutes, or until a knife inserted comes out clean.

Bacon Muffins

Best served warm with a dollop of butter or sour cream.

Serving Size
Makes 6 muffins

Ingredients

1 cup almond flour

2 1/2 Tbsp coconut flour

1 tsp baking powder

1/2 tsp salt

1/2 tsp pepper

2 eggs

2 tsp red wine vinegar

1/4 cup sour cream

1/2 cup grated Cheddar cheese

4 slices bacon, diced

1 Tbsp butter

1/4 cup chopped green onions for garnishing

Directions

1.   Preheat oven to 350°F. Grease a 6-cup muffin tin with non-stick cooking spray.

2.   In a large mixing bowl, add almond flour, coconut flour, baking powder, salt, and pepper and combine with hand or stand mixer.

3.   Add the eggs, red wine vinegar, sour cream, and Cheddar cheese, and mix until just combined. Set aside.

4.   In a medium frying pan, sauté the bacon over medium heat for 5 minutes. Then stir in the butter and allow it to melt.

5.   Add bacon and butter to the mixing bowl, and mix well.

6.   Spoon mixture equally into the muffin tin, forming a peak in the center.

7.   Bake for 15 to 18 minutes, or until a skewer or toothpick inserted comes out clean.

8.   Serve warm, and garnish with chopped green onion.

Bacon, Zucchini, and Mushroom Frittata

Perfect for using leftovers from last night's dinner.

Serving Size

6

Ingredients

8 slices thick-cut bacon, diced into 1-inch cubes

1 1/2 Tbsp butter

1 cup button mushrooms, halved or quartered

1/4 cup grated Parmesan cheese, plus extra for serving

8 eggs, lightly beaten

salt and pepper

1 Tbsp olive oil

2 zucchini, sliced in half circles

Directions

1. Place an oven rack to the second position from the top, and preheat broiler.

2. Heat a large, non-stick, ovenproof frying pan over high heat. Cook the bacon for 3 minutes, or until golden. Then using a slotted spoon, remove and set aside to drain on a paper towel.

3. Reduce the heat to medium. Melt the butter in the pan, and cook the mushrooms until they begin to turn golden. Remove and set aside.

4. In a medium bowl, mix the Parmesan cheese and the eggs. Season mixture with salt and pepper.

5. Heat the olive oil in the pan over medium heat. Pour the egg mixture into the pan, then top with the bacon, mushrooms, and zucchini. Cook for 5 to 10 minutes. Use a rubber spatula to lift the base, allowing liquid eggs to run under until the base is cooked.

6. Place the frittata under the broiler for 3 to 5 minutes, or until the top is set.

7. Spread Parmesan cheese on top to serve.

Baked Eggs in Avocado

Serve with your favorite hot sauce.

Serving Size

6

Ingredients

3 avocados, halved and pitted

6 large eggs

salt and pepper

1/2 tsp smoked paprika

2 Tbsp chopped fresh chives for garnishing

Directions

1. Preheat oven to 425°F. Lightly coat a baking sheet with non-stick cooking spray.

2. Using a spoon, scoop out about 2 Tbsp of avocado flesh from each avocado, creating a small well in the center.

3. One at a time, crack eggs into a small bowl or ramekin, and slide it into the well, keeping the yolk intact. Repeat with remaining eggs. Season with salt, pepper, and paprika to taste.

4. Bake avocados until the egg whites have set, but the yolks are still runny, about 15 to 18 minutes.

5. Garnish with chives, and serve immediately.

Egg Muffins *with Spinach, Bacon, and Cheese*

Hot or cold, these are a real protein boost!

Serving Size

6

Ingredients

8 eggs

1/2 cup milk

1/2 tsp salt

1/4 tsp pepper

2 cups shredded Cheddar cheese

1 (10-ounce) package frozen spinach, thawed and squeezed dry

6 slices bacon, cooked, drained, and chopped

Directions

1. Preheat oven to 350°F. Spray a 12-cup muffin tin with non-stick cooking spray.

2. In a large bowl, beat eggs until smooth. Add milk, salt, pepper, and Cheddar cheese and mix. Stir spinach and cooked bacon into the egg mixture.

3. Ladle the egg mixture into muffin cups until about 3/4 full.

4. Bake for 25 minutes. Remove from the oven, and let the muffins cool before serving.

Blueberry Lemon Smoothie

Delicious smoothies that are easy to make.

Serving Size

2

Ingredients

1 (14-ounce) can unsweetened coconut milk

1/2 cup frozen or fresh blueberries

1 Tbsp lemon juice, plus extra to taste

1/2 tsp vanilla extract

Directions

1. Add coconut milk, blueberries, lemon juice, and vanilla extract to a blender. Blend until smooth.

2. Add more lemon juice, if desired, and pour into a glass to serve.

Green Detox Smoothie

Serving Size

1

Ingredients

1 cup water

2 stalks celery, roughly chopped

1 small pear, cored and diced

4 kale leaves, stemmed

2 handfuls baby spinach

2 to 3 ice cubes (optional)

Directions

1. Pour water into a blender. Add celery, pear, kale, and spinach. Add ice for a colder smoothie, if desired. Blend until smooth.

2. Pour into a glass to serve.

Kale, Mint, and Avocado Smoothie

A healthy but flavorful smoothie option!

Serving Size

2

Ingredients

1/2 avocado, pitted

8 kale leaves, stemmed

1/4 cup fresh mint leaves

1 stalk celery

1/4 small cucumber

1 cup unsweetened almond or coconut milk

1 Tbsp almond butter

1 Tbsp lemon juice

Directions

1. Scoop the flesh out of the avocado.
2. Add kale, mint, avocado, celery, cucumber, almond milk, almond butter, and lemon juice to a blender. Blend until smooth.
3. Pour into a glass to serve.

Keto Pancakes *with Berries and Whipped Cream*

Crispy edges are where you want to be!

Serving Size

4

Ingredients

4 eggs

7 ounces cottage cheese

1 Tbsp psyllium husk powder

4 Tbsp butter or coconut oil

1 cup heavy whipping cream

Serving Suggestions

1/2 cup fresh raspberries

1/2 cup fresh blueberries

1/2 cup fresh strawberries, sliced

Directions

1. Add eggs, cottage cheese, and psyllium husk powder to a medium bowl.

2. Mix together until combined. Let sit for 5 to 10 minutes to thicken.

3. Heat butter in a medium, non-stick skillet. Drop batter about 2 Tbsp at a time onto the skillet, flattening slightly. Fry the pancakes on medium-low heat for 3 to 4 minutes on each side.

4. Meanwhile, whip cream until thick.

5. Serve pancakes topped with whipped cream and desired berries.

Cauliflower Rice

A great side accompaniment to many entrées. Use this recipe for the Cauliflower "Bread" Buns (see page 23) and the Stuffed Peppers (see page 75).

Serving Size

Makes about 3 cups

Ingredients

1 large head cauliflower

2 Tbsp olive oil

Directions

1. Cut the head of cauliflower into quarters, then trim out the inner core from each quarter. Then break apart into large florets.

2. Transfer the cauliflower to the bowl of a food processor. Pulse until completely broken down into rice-sized granules. You can also grate the florets using the large holes of a box grater.

3. Pull out any unprocessed pieces, and set them aside. Transfer the cauliflower rice to another container, and re-process any large pieces.

4. In a large skillet, fry cauliflower rice in olive oil over medium heat. Stir occasionally until cooked, about 10 minutes.

Cauliflower "Bread" Buns

Low-carb, gluten-free cauliflower "bread." Good for sandwiches, burgers, and more!

Serving Size

Makes 4 buns

Ingredients

3 cups Cauliflower Rice (see page 21)

2 large eggs

1/2 cup shredded Parmesan cheese

2 Tbsp almond flour

2 Tbsp coconut flour

1/2 tsp baking powder

1 tsp dried basil

1 tsp white sesame seeds

Directions

1. Preheat oven to 400°F. Grease a baking sheet lined with parchment paper.

2. In a large bowl, combine Cauliflower Rice, eggs, Parmesan cheese, almond flour, coconut flour, baking powder, and basil, and mix well.

3. Place 1/2 cup lightly packed cauliflower mixture onto the prepared baking sheet. Press down on the mixture with the palm of your hand to form a round disc, 4 inches wide and slightly more than 1/2-inch high. Compact the cauliflower mixture gently with your fingers so the cauliflower buns will be tight. Repeat this process until you are out of mix. Sprinkle tops of "bread" buns with sesame seeds.

4. Bake for 20 to 25 minutes, or until tops are golden and cauliflower buns are completely cooked. Use a thin spatula to gently loosen the bottoms of the cauliflower buns from the baking sheet. Allow buns to cool slightly before eating.

Cobb Salad

A great salad dinner for two!

Serving Size

2

Ingredients

2 eggs

3 ounces bacon, diced

5 ounces iceberg lettuce, chopped

1 1/2 cups cooked rotisserie chicken, cubed
or 2 large chicken breasts, cooked and cubed

1 avocado, pitted, peeled, and diced

1 cup quartered cherry tomatoes

1/4 cup blue cheese, crumbled

salt and pepper

Dressing

1 tsp Dijon mustard

1 1/2 Tbsp red wine vinegar

1/4 cup olive oil

salt and pepper

Directions

1. Boil water in a medium saucepan.

2. Place the eggs in boiling water for 8 to 10 minutes. Cool in ice water for easier peeling. Once peeled, roughly chop eggs.

3. In a medium skillet, fry bacon over high heat until crispy. Remove and drain on a paper towel.

4. To make the dressing, add Dijon mustard, red wine vinegar, olive oil, salt, and pepper to a jar. Seal jar with lid, and shake well for 30 seconds.

5. Line a large serving bowl with chopped lettuce, drizzle half the dressing on top, and toss until well coated. Top with rows of egg, chicken, avocado, tomato, blue cheese, and bacon. Season with salt and pepper to taste.

6. Drizzle remaining dressing over top, and toss well just before serving.

Keto Muffins *with Cheddar Cheese*

These will not rise like traditional muffins, but they are a great addition to your brunch table.

Serving Size

Makes 12 muffins

Ingredients

5 large eggs

1/2 tsp salt

1 tsp garlic powder

1/2 tsp cayenne pepper

1 1/2 cups almond flour

1 tsp baking soda

1 tsp chopped thyme leaves

2 cups grated Cheddar cheese

1/2 cup grated Parmesan cheese

Directions

1. Preheat oven to 350°F. Spray a 12-cup muffin tin with non-stick cooking spray.

2. In a large bowl, whisk together the eggs, salt, garlic powder, and cayenne pepper.

3. Stir in the almond flour and baking soda, mixing well. Add the thyme leaves, Cheddar cheese, and Parmesan cheese. Batter will be thick and dough-like but sticky.

4. Using a large scoop, divide the batter evenly between the muffin cups.

5. Bake until golden and a toothpick inserted in center comes out clean, 22 to 25 minutes.

6. Let cool for 5 minutes in the pan, then transfer to a cooling rack to cool for 5 more minutes before serving.

Lettuce Wrap Shrimp Tacos

Shrimp may have a carb count, but it's very low, and the shrimp brings great flavor to this dish!

Serving Size

4

Ingredients

1 pound medium shrimp, peeled and deveined

2 tsp ground cumin

1/2 tsp crushed red pepper flakes

2 Tbsp lime juice

3 cloves garlic, minced

3 Tbsp extra-virgin olive oil

salt and pepper

Romaine lettuce for serving

1 cup quartered cherry tomatoes

1 avocado, pitted, peeled, and cubed

2 Tbsp chopped cilantro for garnishing

Directions

1. In a large bowl, stir together shrimp, cumin, crushed red pepper flakes, lime juice, garlic, and 2 Tbsp olive oil. Season with salt and pepper. Toss until combined, then let marinate in the refrigerator for at least 10 minutes.

2. In a large skillet over medium heat, heat remaining olive oil. Add shrimp and cook until pink, about 2 minutes per side.

3. To assemble the tacos, lay out lettuce leaves and top with tomatoes, avocado, and cooked shrimp. Garnish with cilantro.

Pesto Zoodles

Guests will go crazy for this dish!

Serving Size

4

Ingredients

Pesto

3/4 cup extra-virgin olive oil

2 cups fresh basil leaves (packed)

1/4 cup pine nuts

1 Tbsp lemon juice

1 clove garlic, crushed

1/2 tsp salt

Zoodles

3 medium zucchini

2 tsp extra-virgin olive oil

1 Tbsp lemon zest (about one lemon)

1/4 cup grated Parmesan cheese for garnishing

Directions

1. To make the pesto, combine olive oil, basil leaves, pine nuts, lemon juice, garlic, and salt in a blender, or food processor, and blend until smooth, but not completely blended. Set aside.

2. Using a spiralizer, or mandolin, prepare the zucchini into noodles.

3. Heat olive oil over medium heat in a medium skillet. Add zoodles and lemon zest. Stir in 3/4 cup pesto sauce, and toss to heat through.

4. Serve topped with grated Parmesan cheese.

Tangy Avocado Mayo

Tangy Avocado Mayo can be stored in the refrigerator for 1 week, and Mustard Vinaigrette can be stored for 2 weeks.

Ingredients

1 medium avocado, pitted, peeled, and cubed

1/4 cup extra-virgin olive oil

1 Tbsp lime juice

1 tsp sriracha sauce

salt

Directions

1. Put avocado, olive oil, lime juice, and sriracha sauce into a blender or food processor, and blend until smooth. Add salt to taste.

Mustard Vinaigrette

Ingredients

1 cup olive oil

1/4 cup Dijon mustard

1/4 cup apple cider vinegar

3 cloves garlic, minced (about 1 Tbsp)

1/2 tsp salt

1/2 tsp pepper

Directions

1. Put olive oil, Dijon mustard, vinegar, garlic, salt, and pepper in a jar with a tightly sealed lid. Shake well until the dressing is thickened and oil is emulsified, about 30 seconds.

Zucchini Noodles *with Tomatoes and Feta*

There are so many toppings for zoodles. Here is a Mediterranean version.

Serving Size

2

Ingredients

2 zucchini

2 Tbsp olive oil

1 cup halved cherry tomatoes

2 tsp lemon juice

1 tsp dried oregano

1/4 cup crumbled feta cheese for garnishing

Directions

1. Spiralize the zucchini with a spiralizer or mandolin.

2. In a large saucepan, heat olive oil and add the cherry tomatoes, sautéing until they begin to wilt. Stir in zucchini noodles, lemon juice, and oregano. Stir to heat through, about 1 to 2 minutes.

3. Remove to serving plate, and sprinkle with crumbled feta cheese.

Bacon and Blue Cheese Deviled Eggs

Are you feeling devilish?

Serving Size

6

Ingredients

6 large eggs

1/4 cup sour cream

1/3 cup mayonnaise

1 Tbsp Dijon mustard

salt and pepper

1/4 tsp dried dill

1/4 cup crumbled blue cheese

3 slices cooked bacon, finely chopped

Directions

1. To make perfect hard-boiled eggs, place the eggs in a large saucepan. Add enough cold water that the eggs are fully covered. Over high heat, bring the water to a rolling boil. Once the water is boiling, remove the pan from heat, cover, and let sit for 12 minutes. Run cold water over the eggs and peel.

2. Cut each hard-boiled egg in half. Place the cooked yolk into a medium bowl and the cooked egg white onto an egg plate.

3. Mash the egg yolks with a fork until they resemble coarse crumbs. Mix in the sour cream, mayonnaise, Dijon mustard, salt, and pepper until the mixture is creamy. Stir in the dill, blue cheese, and half of the bacon.

4. Put mixture into a piping bag, or a resealable plastic bag. Squeeze the mixture to one corner of the bag, and snip off that corner. Use this to pipe the mixture back into the egg white halves.

5. Top each egg with the remaining bacon.

Bacon Guacamole Deviled Eggs

Here is how you can love deviled eggs even more!

Serving Size

6

Ingredients

6 large eggs, hard-boiled

1 large avocado, pitted, peeled, and cubed

2 cloves garlic, minced

1 Tbsp lime juice

1/2 tsp salt

pinch of cayenne pepper

4 strips thick-cut bacon, cooked crisp and crumbled

Directions

1. Cut each hard-boiled egg in half. Place the cooked yolk into a medium bowl and the cooked egg white onto an egg plate.

2. Mash the egg yolks with a fork until they resemble coarse crumbs. Add avocado, garlic, lime juice, salt, cayenne pepper, and half of the bacon. Mix until all ingredients are well incorporated.

3. Use a small spoon to put the mixture back into the egg white halves.

4. Top each egg with remaining bacon.

Cauliflower Fritters

Leftover broccoli works, too!

Serving Size

2–4

Ingredients

2 cups cooked cauliflower, finely chopped

1/2 cup thinly sliced scallions

1 Tbsp almond flour

2 eggs

salt and pepper

2 Tbsp butter

1 Tbsp olive oil

sour cream for serving

Directions

1. Press the cauliflower between two paper towels to remove excess moisture. Mix together with scallions, almond flour, eggs, and a dash of salt and pepper in a medium mixing bowl.

2. In a large, non-stick skillet, heat the butter and olive oil over medium-high heat.

3. When hot, add spoonfuls of the cauliflower mixture and flatten out into small pancakes. Fry on each side for 2 to 3 minutes, until golden brown and cooked through.

4. Serve with a dollop of sour cream.

Chicken Satay *with Peanut Sauce*

Start early to give this dish time to marinate.

Serving Size

4

Ingredients

1/2 cup full-fat coconut milk

3 cloves garlic, minced

1/4 tsp cayenne pepper

1/2 tsp salt

1/2 tsp pepper

2 large boneless, skinless chicken breasts (about 1 pound), cut into 1 1/2-inch cubes

lime wedges for serving

Peanut Sauce

1/4 cup natural, smooth peanut butter

2 cloves garlic, grated

1 Tbsp grated ginger

2 Tbsp sesame oil

1 Tbsp soy sauce

1 Tbsp lime juice

1 tsp honey

1 tsp hot sauce

Directions

1. In a large bowl, mix the coconut milk, garlic, cayenne pepper, salt, and pepper. Add the chicken. Stir well to coat. Cover and refrigerate for 4 to 6 hours.

2. Preheat oven to 450°F. Soak 10 wooden skewers in water for about 30 minutes.

3. Thread chicken onto the skewers, leaving about half of each skewer empty for handling. Place them in a single layer on a large baking sheet. Bake for 10 minutes, flip the skewers, and then bake for another 5 minutes, or until cooked through.

4. To make the peanut sauce, add peanut butter, garlic, ginger, sesame oil, soy sauce, lime juice, honey, and hot sauce to a small saucepan. Whisk together over medium-low heat until smooth, about 2 to 3 minutes. Once heated, add water (1 Tbsp at a time), until sauce reaches the desired consistency for dipping. Keep warm over low heat, stirring occasionally.

5. Transfer chicken skewers onto a serving plate, and brush peanut sauce over the chicken. Serve warm with lime wedges and extra sauce on the side for dipping.

Baked Feta *with Olives and Spices*

Feel free to mix up the olives. Now is your chance to check out the deli section of your local grocery.

Serving Size

4 (as an appetizer)

Ingredients

1 cup feta cheese, cubed

1/4 cup extra-virgin olive oil

1 tsp smoked sweet paprika

1 cup whole green olives, pitted

1 Tbsp chopped rosemary

1 Tbsp chopped thyme, plus 2 whole stems for garnishing

1 tsp whole peppercorns

1 tsp sesame seeds

1 Tbsp balsamic vinegar for garnishing

Directions

1. Preheat oven to 350°F.
2. Place the feta cheese in a small, ovenproof dish.
3. Mix olive oil and paprika in a small bowl. Then pour the mixture over the cheese.
4. Distribute the olives around the feta cheese.
5. Sprinkle with the rosemary, thyme, peppercorns, and sesame seeds. Toss to mix.
6. Place 2 thyme leaves on top and place in the oven and bake for about 20 minutes until hot.
7. Remove from oven, and drizzle with balsamic vinegar before serving.

Spicy Grilled Shrimp Skewers

The shrimp can handle 4 cloves of garlic...can you? Of course you can!

Serving Size

6

Ingredients

2 pounds fresh shrimp, shelled and deveined

4 cloves garlic, minced

1/2 tsp cayenne pepper

2 tsp paprika

1/2 cup olive oil

1 Tbsp lemon juice

1/4 tsp hot sauce

Directions

1. Preheat an outdoor grill, or heat a grill pan on the stovetop, on high. Soak 12 wooden skewers in water for about 30 minutes.

2. Add shrimp to a medium bowl.

3. In a small bowl, mix together garlic, cayenne pepper, paprika, olive oil, lemon juice, and hot sauce.

4. Add mixture to the shrimp, and mix well so shrimp is coated.

5. Thread the shrimp onto skewers.

6. Grill the shrimp skewers for 90 seconds on each side, and serve immediately.

Crab Stuffed Mushrooms

A big hit at your next party.

Serving Size

Makes 20 pieces

Ingredients

1 pound cremini mushrooms (about 20 mushrooms)

salt

8 ounces crab meat, picked over and finely chopped

1/2 cup cream cheese, softened

4 cloves garlic, minced

1 tsp oregano

1 Tbsp chopped fresh parsley

2 Tbsp grated Parmesan cheese

Directions

1. Preheat oven to 400°F. Line a baking sheet with parchment paper.

2. Snap and discard stems from mushrooms. With a damp paper towel, clean the top and sides of each mushroom cap. Then place on the prepared baking sheet and sprinkle with salt.

3. In a large mixing bowl, combine crab, cream cheese, garlic, oregano, and parsley and stir until well mixed.

4. Stuff each mushroom cap with the mixture. Evenly sprinkle Parmesan cheese on top of the stuffed mushrooms.

5. Bake until the mushrooms are tender and the stuffing is browned on top, about 30 minutes.

Keto Meatballs

In this recipe, we eliminate the traditional mixture of bread crumbs and milk, substituting heavy cream to add moisture and tenderness to these delicious meatballs.

Serving Size

4

Ingredients

8 ounces 85% lean ground chuck

8 ounces ground pork

1/4 cup grated Parmesan cheese, plus extra for garnishing

1/4 cup heavy cream

1 large egg, beaten

2 Tbsp minced fresh parsley

1 Tbsp finely grated onion

1 clove garlic, grated

salt and pepper

tomato sauce for serving

zucchini noodles for serving

Directions

1. Place a rack in the middle position of oven and preheat to 400°F. Line a baking sheet with parchment paper or foil.

2. In a medium bowl, mix beef and pork well, breaking up larger pieces. You can use a fork or hand mixer for this, but nothing does a better job than washed hands. Mix in the Parmesan cheese, cream, egg, parsley, onion, garlic, salt, and pepper.

3. Lightly oil your hands, and scoop up a small portion, and roll into a round meatball. Place on the prepared baking sheet. Repeat until you have 12 equal-sized meatballs.

4. Bake meatballs for 15 to 20 minutes.

5. Serve with your favorite tomato sauce on top of a bowl of fresh zucchini noodles, and sprinkle with Parmesan cheese.

Mexican Beef Fajitas

A perfect family dinner. Have tortillas handy for those who want them.

Serving Size
4

Ingredients

3 Tbsp olive oil

1/4 cup chopped cilantro, plus extra for garnishing

2 Tbsp lime juice

1 Tbsp Dijon mustard

1 1/2 pounds skirt or flank steak

1 medium red onion, thinly sliced

4 bell peppers, seeded and thinly sliced

2 Tbsp butter

Fajita Seasoning

2 tsp chili powder

1 tsp cumin

1 tsp garlic powder

1 tsp onion powder

1 tsp smoked paprika

1/2 tsp salt

1/4 tsp pepper

Directions

1. To make the fajita seasoning, combine chili powder, cumin, garlic powder, onion powder, paprika, salt, and pepper in a small bowl. Stir well to mix and set aside.

2. In a medium bowl, combine 2 Tbsp olive oil, cilantro, lime juice, Dijon mustard, and 5 tsp Fajita Seasoning. Reserve 1/4 cup of this marinade for topping the cooked steak. Pour remaining marinade into a large resealable bag, and add the steak. Evenly distribute the marinade, and let sit.

3. Heat remaining olive oil in a large skillet over medium-high heat. Add the onions and cook until softened. Add the bell peppers, and sprinkle with remaining fajita seasoning. Cook until the peppers reach your desired level of softness, and remove vegetables from skillet.

4. Melt butter in the same skillet. As it melts, remove steak from marinade, pat dry, and add to skillet. Sear on both sides for about 3 to 4 minutes. Remove from skillet, and allow to rest for 5 minutes. Then slice against the grain into thin strips.

5. Return steak strips to skillet, along with the onion and bell peppers and add the reserved steak marinade. Stir to heat through.

Chicken Hasselback *Stuffed with Spinach*

A fancy entrée for two. So simple!

Serving Size

2

Ingredients

2 boneless, skinless chicken breasts

1/2 tsp salt, plus extra for seasoning

1/2 tsp pepper, plus extra for seasoning

1 cup spinach, cooked

1/4 cup crumbled goat cheese

1/4 tsp nutmeg

1/4 cup shredded mozzarella cheese

Directions

1. Preheat oven to 400°F. Line a rimmed baking sheet with parchment paper, or grease a baking sheet.

2. Using a sharp knife, make slits in the chicken breasts about 3/4-inch apart, making sure not to cut all the way down through the bottom. Season with salt and pepper.

3. In a medium bowl, mix the spinach and goat cheese together with nutmeg, salt, and pepper.

4. Place the chicken breasts on prepared baking sheet. Stuff the spinach mixture in the slits of the chicken, over-stuffing slightly. Sprinkle the mozzarella cheese on top of each chicken breast.

5. Bake for 25 to 30 minutes, or until the chicken is cooked through. If desired, switch the oven to broil for the last 5 to 10 minutes to brown the cheese.

Butter Chicken

You can use chicken thighs if that is what you have.

Serving Size

4

Ingredients

1 1/2 pounds chicken breast (about 3), cut into 2-inch pieces

2 Tbsp garam masala

3 tsp grated ginger

2 cloves garlic, minced

1/2 cup plain yogurt

1 Tbsp coconut oil

1/2 cup heavy cream

2 Tbsp ghee or butter

salt

chopped cilantro for garnishing

Cauliflower Rice (see page 21) for serving (optional)

Sauce

1 onion, chopped

2 tsp grated ginger

1 clove garlic, minced

1 (14 1/2-ounce) can crushed tomatoes

1 Tbsp ground coriander

1/2 Tbsp garam masala

1 tsp ground cumin

1 tsp chili powder

Directions

1. In a large bowl, add chicken, garam masala, ginger, garlic, and yogurt. Stir to combine. Place in the refrigerator to chill for at least 30 minutes.

2. To make the sauce, place the onion, ginger, garlic, tomatoes, coriander, garam masala, cumin, and chili powder in a blender, and blend until smooth. Set aside.

3. Heat coconut oil over medium-high heat in a large skillet. Place the chicken along with the marinade, in the skillet to brown, about 3 to 4 minutes per side. Once browned, pour in the sauce, and cook for 5 to 6 more minutes, or until chicken is cooked.

4. Stir in the heavy cream and ghee, and continue to cook for 1 minute. Add salt to taste.

5. Top with cilantro and serve with Cauliflower Rice, if desired.

Taco Casserole

Check your taco seasoning label for carb levels.

Serving Size

6

Ingredients

1 Tbsp extra-virgin olive oil

1/2 yellow onion, diced

2 pounds ground beef

2 Tbsp taco seasoning mix (about 1/2 package)

1 jalapeño, seeded and minced, plus 1 jalapeño thinly sliced for serving

6 large eggs, lightly beaten

2 cups grated Monterey Jack cheese

2 Tbsp chopped cilantro for garnishing

1 cup sour cream for serving

Directions

1. Preheat oven to 350°F.

2. In a large skillet over medium heat, heat olive oil and add onion. Cook until onion is slightly softened.

3. Add the ground beef and cook, breaking up the meat until it is no longer pink, about 6 to 7 minutes. Sprinkle in taco seasoning and jalapeño, and cook, stirring, for 1 minute. Strain and let cool slightly.

4. In a large mixing bowl, whisk eggs. Then add meat mixture.

5. Spread mixture into an even layer in the bottom of a large baking dish. Sprinkle with Monterey Jack cheese.

6. Bake until set, about 25 minutes.

7. Sprinkle with cilantro, and top each slice with a dollop of sour cream and jalapeño.

Spinach Stuffed Meatloaf

Lots of steps, but they are simple. You can do it!

Serving Size

6

Ingredients

2 pounds ground beef

2 eggs

3 green onions, whites chopped and greens discarded

3 cloves garlic, minced

1 yellow onion, chopped

1/4 tsp cayenne pepper

1/2 tsp oregano

1/2 tsp salt

1/2 tsp pepper

1 (10-ounce) package frozen spinach, thawed and squeezed dry

4 ounces goat cheese

1/4 tsp nutmeg

2 Tbsp tomato paste

1/2 cup halved cherry tomatoes

1/4 cup grated Parmesan cheese

Directions

1. Preheat oven to 425°F. Line a loaf pan with parchment paper and grease well.

2. In a medium bowl, combine beef, eggs, green onions, garlic, and onion. Mix well to combine. Add cayenne pepper, oregano, salt, and pepper, and mix again.

3. In a different medium mixing bowl, combine the spinach, goat cheese, and nutmeg.

4. Lay out plastic wrap on the counter and then roll the meat mixture on top of it into an 8-inch-wide rectangle.

5. Spread the spinach and goat cheese mixture along the middle.

6. Picking up one side of the plastic wrap, wrap one third of the meat mixture over top of the spinach, then do the same to the other side, laying it on top of the meat. Pinch the top seam and ends closed so the filling stays inside while cooking.

7. Using the plastic wrap as a sling, transfer the meatloaf into the loaf pan.

8. Using a spoon, smear the top of the meatloaf with tomato paste and top with cherry tomatoes and Parmesan cheese.

9. Cook for about 50 to 60 minutes, until the middle is 160°F.

Salmon and Asparagus Packets

Make sure you have foil on hand before you begin.

Serving Size

4

Ingredients

16 asparagus spears, trimmed

4 six-ounce skin-on salmon fillets

4 Tbsp butter

1 lemon, thinly sliced

pepper

fresh dill for garnishing

Directions

1. Preheat oven to 400°F.

2. Lay a large piece of foil on a flat surface. Place 4 spears of asparagus on the foil and top them with 1 fillet of salmon, 1 Tbsp butter, 1 lemon slice, and a sprinkle of pepper. Fold and wrap the foil, sealing it well. Repeat with remaining ingredients until you have 4 packets.

3. Place the 4 packets on a baking sheet and bake for 15 to 20 minutes, until salmon is cooked through and asparagus is tender.

4. Garnish with dill and serve.

Roasted Chicken Thighs

This dish starts in a skillet on the stovetop and finishes in a hot oven. So make sure your skillet can make the journey!

Serving Size

4

Ingredients

8 skin-on chicken thighs

1 Tbsp dried basil

2 Tbsp grated Parmesan cheese

1 tsp chopped rosemary

2 cloves garlic, minced

1/4 tsp salt

1/4 tsp pepper

1 Tbsp olive oil

Directions

1. Preheat oven to 450°F.

2. Trim excess skin and fat from chicken thighs.

3. Using your fingers, or the end of a spoon, create a pocket between the skin and thigh meat and set aside.

4. Mix together basil, Parmesan cheese, rosemary, garlic, salt, pepper, and a few drops of olive oil.

5. Evenly divide the mixture and stuff into the pocket between the chicken skin and thigh meat.

6. Heat remaining olive oil in an ovenproof skillet over medium-high heat.

7. Place chicken thighs skin-side down in the hot skillet and cook for 5 minutes. Flip the thighs and continue cooking on the stovetop for an additional 5 minutes.

8. Transfer skillet to preheated oven, baking for 20 to 25 minutes, or until chicken is cooked through.

9. Let rest for 5 minutes before serving.

Spaghetti Squash Lasagna

No noodles? No problem!

Serving Size

6

Ingredients

1 large spaghetti squash

1 Tbsp olive oil

1 tsp salt

1 pound ground beef

24 ounces marinara sauce (store-bought or homemade)

8 ounces ricotta cheese

1/2 cup grated Parmesan cheese

Directions

1. Preheat oven to 400°F. Line a rimmed baking sheet with parchment paper and rub with olive oil. Spray a 9-by-13-inch baking dish with non-stick cooking spray.

2. Cut the spaghetti squash in half lengthwise. Scoop out the seeds and discard. Drizzle the inside of the squash with olive oil and sprinkle with salt. Place spaghetti squash flesh-side down on the prepared baking sheet and bake for 1 hour, or until fork tender.

3. Use a fork to scrape out long strands of squash, scraping across the width of the squash. Lower oven temperature to 350°F.

4. Meanwhile, brown the ground beef over medium heat in a large skillet.

5. Pour off fat, if there is excess, and add the marinara sauce. Cook for 5 minutes over low heat to heat through.

6. In a medium bowl, mix the ricotta and Parmesan cheeses together and set aside.

7. Place the cooked and scraped spaghetti squash in the prepared baking dish.

8. Top the squash with the meat sauce, then the ricotta cheese mixture.

9. Bake for 20 minutes, or until cheese is browned and casserole is hot. Serve immediately.

Cashew Chicken

Nuts are your friends—even buttery cashews!

Serving Size

4

Ingredients

3/4 cup roasted, unsalted cashews

1/4 cup water

2 tsp almond meal

1 1/2 pounds boneless, skinless chicken breast, cut into 1 1/2-inch pieces

1/2 tsp salt

1/4 tsp pepper

2 Tbsp avocado oil

6 cloves garlic, minced

8 green onions, whites finely chopped and greens roughly chopped for garnishing

2 Tbsp rice wine vinegar

1 Tbsp gluten-free soy sauce

1/4 tsp sesame oil

Directions

1. Preheat oven to 350°F.

2. Place the cashews on a baking sheet and roast in the oven for about 5 minutes, until just starting to change color. Then set aside.

3. Meanwhile, in a small bowl, whisk together the water and almond meal. Then set aside.

4. Put the chicken in a large bowl and sprinkle with salt and pepper.

5. In a large, non-stick skillet, heat 1 Tbsp avocado oil over high heat until very hot. Add half of the chicken to the skillet and stir-fry until lightly browned, but not cooked through, about 3 minutes. Transfer to a plate.

6. Add the remaining avocado oil to the same skillet, and add the remaining chicken, garlic, and onion whites. Stir-fry until the chicken is lightly browned, but not cooked through, about 3 minutes. Return the first batch of chicken to the skillet. Turn the heat down to medium, and add the rice wine vinegar. Cook until evaporated, about 30 seconds.

7. Add the almond meal mixture and soy sauce to the chicken. Cook, tossing, until the chicken is cooked through and coated with sauce, about 3 minutes.

8. Remove from heat and stir in the cashews and sesame oil.

9. Sprinkle with onion greens, and serve immediately.

Pan Seared Lamb Chops

This dish needs at least 4 hours to marinate, so start early!

Serving Size

2

Ingredients

2 cloves garlic, minced

1 Tbsp rosemary, minced

2 tsp Dijon mustard

2 Tbsp olive oil

1 pound lamb chops, trimmed of excess fat

salt and pepper

Directions

1. Combine the garlic and rosemary in a small mixing bowl with the Dijon mustard and 1 Tbsp olive oil.

2. Place the lamb chops in a single layer in a shallow baking dish and season all sides with salt and pepper. Smear the marinade oil on both sides of each lamb chop.

3. Cover with plastic wrap and refrigerate for at least 4 hours.

4. Once marinated, remove from the refrigerator and bring the lamb to room temperature, about 30 minutes.

5. Heat a large frying pan over medium-high heat. When hot, add remaining olive oil, swirling to coat the pan. Add the lamb chops in a single layer, and turn heat down to medium.

6. Let the lamb chops cook, undisturbed, for 6 to 7 minutes. Turn and cook again for another 6 to 7 minutes, depending on how rare you like your lamb chops.

7. Remove the lamb chops and cover loosely with foil. Let sit for 5 minutes before serving.

Shrimp Scampi *with Zoodles*

In this recipe, "scampi" refers to the preparation of the shrimp.

Serving Size

2

Ingredients

2 medium zucchini

1/2 Tbsp unsalted butter

2 tsp extra-virgin olive oil

4 cloves garlic, minced

8 ounces large shrimp (about 12 shrimp), peeled and deveined

salt and pepper

1 Tbsp chopped fresh parsley

1/2 tsp lemon zest (zest before juicing)

3 Tbsp lemon juice

1/8 tsp crushed red pepper flakes

Directions

1. Use a mandolin fitted with a julienne blade, or a spiralizer, to cut the zucchini into noodles.

2. In a large, non-stick pan, melt the butter and 1 tsp olive oil over medium heat. Add 2 tsp garlic and sauté for 1 minute.

3. Add the shrimp, salt, and pepper, and sauté, stirring often, until the shrimp have just turned pink, about 5 minutes. Remove shrimp and set aside.

4. Add the remaining olive oil and garlic to the pan, and cook for 30 seconds. Then add the zucchini noodles and more salt and pepper. Cook, stirring, for 2 minutes.

5. Remove from heat, and add the cooked shrimp, parsley, lemon zest, lemon juice, and crushed red pepper flakes. Toss well to combine and serve immediately.

Stuffed Peppers

Here is another opportunity to use Cauliflower Rice (see page 21).

Serving Size

6

Ingredients

2 Tbsp extra-virgin olive oil

1 pound ground beef

1 tsp dried oregano

1 tsp paprika

1 tsp salt

1/4 tsp pepper

1 medium onion, chopped

3 cloves garlic, minced

1 Tbsp tomato paste

1 (14 1/2-ounce) can diced tomatoes

1 1/2 cups Cauliflower Rice (see page 21)

6 bell peppers, tops and cores removed

1 cup shredded Monterey Jack cheese

Directions

1. Preheat oven to 400°F. Coat a medium baking dish with oil.

2. In a large skillet, heat olive oil over medium-high heat. Add the beef, oregano, paprika, salt, and pepper, and brown for 5 to 7 minutes.

3. Add the onion and garlic, and cook for another 4 to 5 minutes, until the onion starts to soften.

4. Add the tomato paste, tomatoes, and Cauliflower Rice. Cook for 5 minutes.

5. Place the peppers in the prepared baking dish, and divide the mixture evenly between them. Top each pepper with Monterey Jack cheese.

6. Cover with foil, and bake for 30 minutes.

7. Uncover, and bake for another 10 minutes, until the cheese is bubbly.

8. Remove from oven and allow to cool for 5 minutes before serving.

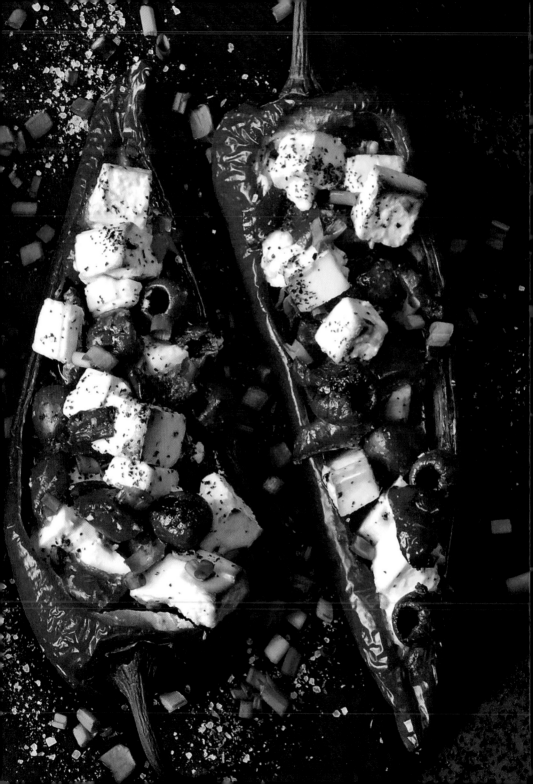

Roasted Red Peppers *with Feta and Olives*

Shepherd peppers are available in September, otherwise use the peppers we have year-round.

Serving Size
2

Ingredients

2 large sweet red peppers, halved and seeded

2 Tbsp extra-virgin olive oil

1/2 cup halved cherry tomatoes

1/2 cup green olives, pitted

1/2 cup cubed feta cheese

2 green onions, sliced

salt and pepper

Directions

1.   Preheat oven to 400° F.

2.   Place peppers in a medium roasting dish. Drizzle with 1 Tbsp olive oil, and roast for 15 minutes.

3.   Fill the peppers with cherry tomatoes, green olives, and feta cheese. Sprinkle with green onion, salt, and pepper, and drizzle with remaining olive oil.

4.   Return to the oven and bake for another 10 to 15 minutes.

Chocolate Peanut Butter Balls

When you just need a treat!

Serving Size

Makes approximately 16 pieces

Ingredients

8 ounces cream cheese, softened to room temperature

1/2 cup natural, smooth peanut butter

1/4 cup plus 2 Tbsp coconut oil

pinch of salt

1 cup keto-friendly dark chocolate chips

Directions

1. Line a baking sheet with parchment paper.

2. In a medium bowl, combine the cream cheese, peanut butter, 1/4 cup coconut oil, and salt. Using a hand mixer, beat mixture until fully combined. Place the bowl in freezer for about 10 minutes.

3. When peanut butter mixture has hardened, use a tablespoon to create peanut butter balls and place on baking sheet. Place in refrigerator to harden for 5 minutes.

4. Meanwhile, combine chocolate chips and remaining coconut oil in a microwave-safe bowl. Microwave in 30-second intervals until fully melted.

5. Pour melted chocolate over peanut butter balls, covering completely and allowing the excess chocolate to pool on the baking sheet. Place in refrigerator to harden for 5 minutes.

6. Serve once hardened, or keep covered in the refrigerator.

Considering a keto diet? Try some of these recipes to decide if this way of eating is for you. If the whole plan is not for you, you may still enjoy incorporating some of these dishes into your menu planning.